AF130189

NOTHING HAPPENS BY CHANCE

NOTHING HAPPENS BY CHANCE

7 RULES FOR SUCCESSFUL LIVING

Neil A. Mence

Copyright 2011 by Neil A. Mence

All rights reserved.

WRITINGS BY NEIL A. MENCE:

<u>Self-development</u>:

Successful Living

Nothing Happens by Chance – 7 Rules for Successful Living

The Affirmation Handbook (Volumes 1 and 2)

The Royal Road to Abundant Living (co-authored)

Get a Life (available as an eBook)

<u>Metaphysical:</u>

The Greatest Stories Ever Told
(A metaphysical interpretation of the Old Testament)

<u>General interest:</u>

Health and Reincarnation

PREFACE

We live in an incredibly complex and mind-puzzling universe. Each time science believes it has an explanation another seemingly impossible-to-answer question pops up. Why is there more gravitational pull in the universe than visible matter can account for? Where is all this 'missing' matter? Why do galaxies pick up speed as they move away from one another? Why is space flat, rather than curved, in the absence of matter? Why is it that seemingly 'invisible' space is actually teeming with activity that we can't see?

The common denominator is 'energy'. And, as the First Law of Thermodynamics states, energy can never be created or destroyed; it can only be transformed (changed from one form to another).

But what is this energy? At the human level we know what it does because we can see and measure its effects by physical exertion. On the cosmic plane we can also quantify its outputs and impacts. But, are we any closer to understanding its real essence?

In 2009 the Large Hadron Collider at Cern, Switzerland, was activated in an attempt to resolve inconsistencies in theoretical physics and to test various predictions including the existence of the Higgs Boson, commonly referred to as the 'God particle'. The Collider is being used to help explain the origin of mass in the universe and to perhaps answer that age-old question, "How did the universe come to be the way it is?" Perhaps some light will be shed on the questions that each of us has.

For thousands of years mankind has believed that energy (which some call 'spirit') is the invisible essence or life-force behind all physical form. And since logic dictates that there can't be one type of energy working at the cosmic or universal level and another type on the human plane, it stands to reason that energy exists everywhere, not just in some parts of the universe, and that it expresses itself in various forms.

We can reasonably deduce from this that everything is energy either in form (the seemingly visible) or the unformed (the seemingly invisible). But how does energy know what form to take? Is universal energy self-directing or must it be directed?

We know that our physical bodies encompass a life-force which flows through us from what we call the moment of birth until the moment of death; it's what animates and triggers the various systems within our bodies. It's what we call the "I" of "I am" and we know from our actions and reactions, moods, feelings and emotions, that it's causative – when we feel okay we attract more to be happy about and when we're feeling down in the dumps, we attract even more negative feelings.

So is there a connection between universal energy and this internal life-force which we use either consciously or unconsciously every second of our lives? Undoubtedly, and science is seeking answers.

In the meantime we're left with the observation that what scientists call energy, psychologists call mind, philosophers call reality, and religionists call God, all amount to the same thing – an ever-present energy which can change form according to the direction given it. In us humans that direction is through our thoughts which choose what to believe and accept, and what not to believe or accept.

Accordingly, nothing happens by chance in our lives; all is related to the direction we give universal energy through our thoughts and feelings. It's our individual choice as to whether to use this universal energy by design or by default.

TABLE OF CONTENTS

INTRODUCTION

"How's life treating you?" Do you remember the last time someone asked you that? Each time I hear that question I can't help but feel that the person asking somehow believes that life is a game of chance and that things just 'happen'; that we have no say in what is happening to us.

Fortunately life isn't like that at all; in fact it's quite the opposite. The truth is that nothing happens in life by chance. Things don't just happen -- they happen because of what goes on inside of us. We continually attract things and experiences into our lives through the thoughts, feelings, beliefs, words and vibrations that we're sending out. The greatest truism of life is that what we put out we always get back; and that includes our thoughts and feelings, as well as our actions. Chapter 1 explains more fully this first rule of successful living.

The truth, however, is that most of us are searching for that elusive 'something' which we think will make us feel happier and more fulfilled. There isn't a person on the face of the earth who hasn't at some time dreamed of having more love, peace of mind, health, money or some other 'thing' that they genuinely believe will make them feel happier and more 'complete'. And in this fast-paced world we usually want it right now!

The basic rules governing the action of life are straightforward. To live life effectively we need to learn how to attract the experiences we truly want, rather than those we don't want.

Understanding the truth about living a successful life is the easy part; it's the 'doing' part that most of us have difficulty with because no one can do it for us and we usually look for an easy way out. Each of us must come to the realisation in our own time that we have choices and that it takes practice, practice and more practice to succeed. No one sitting down at a grand piano for the first time can give a faultless concert performance. We all understand that years of practice go into giving a perfectly faultless recital.

It all boils down to commitment; a commitment not only to ensuring that our habitual thoughts are in fact affirmations and an acceptance of the good we truly want, but to firmly believing that the desired good is already ours right at this moment. It's a life-long process.

For each of us our aim is to experience more of the good things in life -- improved health, greater abundance, better relationships and a more fulfilling self-expression. Nothing happens by chance! Everything, absolutely everything, manifests according to our mental equivalents -- OUR mental equivalents, not those of anyone else!

The ideas in this book aren't new; they've been known for thousands of years. But here in this small volume the reader will find an explanation of how things work, how they get to be the way they are, and how we can use universal energy to continuously live in the flow of peace, harmony, love, prosperity and health.

I sincerely trust that this book's simplicity conveys a message and idea that the reader will find easy to follow and to apply.

Neil A. Mence
London, England
2011

Chapter 1

HOW THINGS GET TO BE THE WAY THEY ARE

"For to him who has, will more be given,
and he will have abundance; but from him
who has not, even what he has will be taken away."
(Matthew 13:12)

Strange words! Words that have often been misunderstood; words that might inspire or conspire to bring hope or fear. Many have questioned their fairness, believing they mean that the rich get richer and the poor get poorer. Nothing could be further from the truth!

First things first

Let's start, however, by cutting through the cobwebs of ambiguity and getting right to the heart of the matter. Once and for all we must get rid of the idea that things happen to us because of what is happening around us; that we're like a cork in the ocean being pushed first one way and then another; that we have no control over the events in our lives.

The truth is that each of us is living a life of choice. It's up to each of us in the quietness of our own mind to accept and use this knowledge and to make changes, or to reject it and perhaps live a life chequered with lack, limitation or ill health; one in which there perhaps appears to be no love and no hope.

The rule -- that one fundamental principle upon which each child should be reared -- the reality that each of us must consciously hold in our mind every second, is that everything happens to us, and in our lives, because of the way we think and the conviction or degree of belief that accompanies our thoughts. In other words, our experiences are a reflection of our consciousness.

The quote at the beginning of this Chapter refers to consciousness -- "To him who has (in consciousness) will more be given". In other words, if we have a consciousness of unlimited abundance, more will be given to us. But those who do not have (in consciousness) "…even what he has will be taken away." This is the same as saying that if we have a consciousness of lack, the little that we do have will be reduced or taken away from us because of our limiting thoughts.

What we think, feel and believe is the magnet that attracts things to us. It's not just the thoughts alone that are important, but the beliefs and feelings, or degree of conviction that accompanies the thoughts. Thoughts and feelings of worry, fear, lack, limitation and unworthiness, or of being unloved and unwanted, result in the manifestation of even greater levels of limitation.

Happily, the opposite is true and thoughts of love, peace and abundance that are believed in will result in the appearance of an even greater profusion of those things in our lives.

Most of us probably don't want to accept that we've attracted everything and everyone that's in our life but let's be realistic. We can't get away from ourselves. Wherever we go we take our mind with us so regardless of where we are, we're always thinking the same thoughts until we choose to change them. That's why it comes as a shock to many people when they hear for the first time that it's their thoughts and beliefs that cause the illness, poverty or unhappiness that they're experiencing.

Cause and Effect

Up to this point we've been talking about the great Law of Life, better known as the Law of Cause and Effect. And like all laws, whether they be spiritual or physical (such as the laws of mathematics, gravity or electricity), the Law of Cause and Effect is at work in all places at all times.

The trap into which many of us have fallen is in not understanding the process involved in the Law of Life. We look at an effect and, deciding that we want something different, we try to change the effect rather than looking for the cause and changing that. For example, poor health and financial restriction are effects and many people try to treat the symptoms, which are effects, instead of looking at what caused the effect. Masking symptoms may work in the short term but unless the cause is addressed, the effects will continue to manifest.

This brings us back to the state of our consciousness. Whatever we have in consciousness (in other words, whatever we believe) is true for us. This is what is known as a 'conditioned consciousness.' Once again we should remember the quotation at the beginning of chapter, "To him who hath (in consciousness), will more be given… but from him who has not (in consciousness) even what he has will be taken away."

Whatever the effect is that we want to change, we must first examine the cause by asking ourselves questions such as, "What have I been thinking about in regard to this matter?" What we should **not** be doing is examining the effect by asking questions or making statements such as, "Did I spend too much?" "Was I too wasteful?" "Other people let me down". These are only effects from the causes we've sown within our consciousness. We, and we alone, are responsible for the causes that produce the results that we don't like.

We always need to be careful about what we're thinking and feeling. As shown in the following example, impatiently held thoughts can produce seemingly negative results.

Isn't patience a great thing?

Sometimes a personal trait is long overlooked until something drastic happens to make us sit up and take note. This is what happened to Richard from Ottawa, Canada, who was well known for his impatience, always wanting to have things done in a hurry.

One day, a small act of impatience led to a major event that, while it may not have turned him into the most patient person in the world certainly made him look at himself and helped temper his brusqueness. It's one of those stories that we sometimes see on television or read about; a story of false accusation or perhaps mistaken identity to which we might say, "How terrible", "That can't happen in real life," or "That couldn't happen to me."

Well it can happen -- it happened to this businessman.
Being accused of trying to kill someone is not a thing that many of us would take lightly. Just think about it. How would you react if you were suddenly confronted by a police officer at your front door with a warrant charging you with criminal negligence, dangerous driving and what was tantamount to attempted murder?

That is exactly what happened to Richard -- what had started out as a minor traffic incident several months previously had suddenly exploded into a major situation. In a state of shock he tried to recall what'd happened -- he'd stopped at some road construction and, being impatient, had turned his car around to go another route. In the process, however, he'd accidentally knocked over a small orange marker on the road.

A construction worker who saw this jumped in his truck, followed Richard and got out and verbally abused him when stopped at a traffic light. Reaching into Richard's car he grabbed his tie screaming obscenities. Fortunately the light turned green and Richard slammed his foot down and drove off leaving the other man shouting in the middle of the road.

A series of false accusations followed and the next six months were among the worst in Richard's life. With the help of friends a criminal lawyer was hired and prayer and support groups formed. Then a one day trial had to be extended when time ran out.

The testimony given during the first day of the trial would have been laughable if it weren't so serious. Three of the prosecution's witnesses gave different stories. Each said a car had bumped into one of their co-workers but three different types and colour of car were described and it was claimed that the so-called culprit had left in three different directions.

The third witness, a burly man a foot taller than Richard and weighing at least 100 lbs more, said he'd caught his coat in Richard's car door when he'd gone to speak to him and had been dragged along one of Canada's busiest highways for several miles.

He then started to choke whilst on the witness stand and couldn't continue.

The next day the case was held over for another month because this "important" prosecution witness was too ill. One month later it was announced to the court that this gentleman was in hospital, his face swollen and paralysed, his jaw locked and he'd lost his ability to speak. The prosecution withdrew the charge and Richard walked out of the court room crying from relief and joy that the whole thing was over.

What is important here is not only that truth prevailed, but the lesson learned. At the time Richard certainly did not think along the lines that his thoughts and actions had attracted that particular result but, as he later realised, his impatiently-held thoughts and attitudes toward life had set up a field of attraction around him that was bound to produce unwanted results.

As Richard later said, "Now, when I read or hear of people being released after spending years in jail for a crime that new evidence such as DNA testing proves they were not guilty of, I can feel an empathy and compassion that previously I'd not have thought possible. I've been there. I believe that what happened to me certainly helped me to change the way I think."

It can't be emphasized enough

The main Law of Life is that whatever we think, feel and believe sets in motion something that's as certain and as real as physical laws. It follows, therefore, that we must continually be aware of our thoughts and actions and to know that by thinking and believing a certain way we develop a corresponding consciousness which acts as a magnet attracting similar things to itself.

Once we realise what causes our conditions we can change the cause, thereby changing the conditions to something that we do want to experience. It's a message that has been stated repeatedly by word and in literature:

- "It is done unto you as you believe."

- "Thoughts become the things thought about all day."

- "We always reap what we sow."

- "What goes around, comes around."

From the foregoing, we can determine the great equation of life:

$$T + B = C$$

(**T**hought + **B**elief = **C**ause which results in the effect we experience).

This is how life adds up. Keep this equation in mind as you continue. Einstein had $E = MC^2$ and we have $T + B = C$ as an equation for taking control of our lives.

POINTS TO REFLECT UPON

1. Life is consciousness. It's what goes on in our mind that counts, NOT what we say or do. Life is a reflection of the thoughts we think and believe because, like a magnet, they set up vibrations which attract things similar to them.

2. Each of us must learn to take charge of our own life. We do this by taking responsibility for our thoughts – and that includes the idle chatter that goes on in our minds all the time, the conversations we have with ourselves, the gossip in which we may indulge with others, and our habitual thoughts. We alone are responsible for what we experience.

3. We must look at what we DO want, NOT at what we don't want. For example, if money is needed, we work on gaining a consciousness of abundance and prosperity. By saying or thinking that it's needed or wanted we believe we don't have it and so, through the Law of Life, we'll get more of the same (i.e. more belief that we don't have).

4. Does it shock you to realise that your affirmations and prayers are being answered exactly as you have believed they would be? Thoughts of lack and limitation result in a greater abundance of lack and limitation while thoughts of love, abundance and peace result in that which is truly desired. What we think and feel either limits or expands our good.

5. When you ask for something do you truly expect to get it or do you say "I hope" that it'll materialise? Expectation is thought coupled with a definite belief that a thing already is. Hope is devoid of belief and so, like armchair faith, goes with the wind.

6. The great equation of life is T + B = C (thought added to belief creates a cause which results in an effect). Since an effect follows cause as definitely as day follows night we can choose the effects we want to experience by establishing specific patterns in our thoughts.

7. Our lives are a continual expression of the process of the Law of Cause and Effect. We understand, therefore, that adverse experiences are valuable in that they're an indication of incorrect beliefs or thoughts. We now know that we have to change our thoughts and feelings to have the effect altered!

Chapter 2

LIFE'S AN INSIDE JOB

"...there is nothing good or bad, but thinking makes it so".
(Hamlet: Act 2, scene 2)

If nothing happens by chance, then logic dictates that everything is in our life because we have somehow attracted it either consciously or unconsciously through our thoughts and beliefs.

As we learned in Chapter 1, life is really a reflection of our consciousness. Sooner or later we must come to the realisation that each of us experiences exactly what we expect to experience, exactly what we believe. Please note that I said 'expect'; I didn't say 'wish' or 'want'.

The whole secret lies in getting into the realisation that we can only experience what we expect, what we believe, what we continually give our attention to. **The Law of Life can only respond to the direction we give it**.

"But", some readers cry out, "I didn't ask for, or expect, things to turn out as they have." No, but perhaps the possibility of what you didn't want was in your mind and you gave attention to it by saying something like, "I hope it doesn't happen."

It's often a subtle process of mind. A woman from London, England, told me how for years she'd run a successful graphic arts business when suddenly the orders stopped coming in, the bills started to pile up and her financial future appeared to be very bleak. Her accountant, perhaps thinking she was offering a way out from the financial burden, suggested her client declare bankruptcy. "No!" she exclaimed, "Never!"

As time passed she found herself stating over and over that she would not declare bankruptcy. But, just as Job said "... the thing which I greatly feared is come upon me" (Job 3:25), she was forced into bankruptcy. It took several years for her to regain her self-respect and to grow into the realisation that through accepting the idea of bankruptcy she had attracted it to her.

By directing personal thought and choosing only those things we want to experience in life, plus having the expectancy of receiving, we attract our desires. By dwelling on the negative, or speaking about the things we don't want, we give them life and power and often end up experiencing them.

The universal Law of Cause and Effect is always in operation, not just sometimes and not just in some places, but everywhere at the same time! To emphasise what we already know, thought combined with belief are the two constituent parts of causation. We need to learn how to use both elements correctly so that our experiences are joyous, healthy and prosperous. Let's take a closer look at each.

Thought

Thought is the activity of our mind -- that great mental computer which is so personal to each of us. We alone choose which programs (i.e. thoughts) we run with this computer -- thoughts of peace and prosperity or thoughts of lack and limitation; thoughts of happiness and health or thoughts of fear and anxiety.

Thought has been called the great director – it's the mechanism by which we choose what we want and what we don't want in our lives. Through thought our imagination can soar to unlimited heights; our mind always achieves what it imagines and believes.

References are sometimes made to various types of thought -- trained/guided, untrained, and habitual. An understanding of each is worthwhile.

Trained/guided thoughts are, as implied, thoughts directed along a specific line of intent to experience a desired result. For example, if we're seeking to improve our health, all thoughts are focussed on the idea of perfect health. We would in fact be training or guiding our thoughts to see, know, understand and acknowledge only perfect health within ourselves.

12

Untrained thoughts are those that flit across our mind without direction and are often affected by race consciousness. Untrained thinking occurs when we're not deliberately focusing on something we want to manifest or experience. This means that most of the time we're at the mercy of race consciousness, much like a small plane that's buffeted around when it gets caught up in the jet stream of a larger plane.

Habitual thoughts are the chitchat or small talk that continually goes on in our mind. Most of the time we're not consciously guiding these regularly-held thoughts which are responsible for forming our consciousness They're the thoughts that attract the events and experiences into our lives which mirror exactly our inner habitual and untrained thoughts and feelings.

The process of altering unwanted conditions in our lives involves using trained thoughts to think in a specific way so that they automatically become our habitual way of thinking. Habitual thoughts, combined with belief, always produce results.

Someone once said that if you want to understand the quality of your thoughts, think like a gardener. Like gardeners we can only produce from the seeds that we've sown. So let's ask ourselves, "What kind of seeds am I sowing at this moment?"

Belief

Belief is the energy (conviction, faith, power) which, when combined with thought, produces results. The stronger the belief, the more convinced we are, the more likely and the more quickly will results materialise.

It's at this point that many people go wrong. They pray or make an affirmative statement and when nothing appears to happen complain that, "My prayers aren't being answered". We need always to keep in mind the quotation at the top of Chapter 1, "For to him who has ...." (in consciousness). How quickly we forget!

Belief is the producer. We can sit all day saying, "I want a new car", or affirm that, "I am healthy, I am healthy, I am healthy now." But nothing, absolutely nothing, will happen until the thought is believed, until we totally accept the thought with all our being, until all else disappears from our mind but an absolute certainty in that thought or spoken statement.

If we make a claim for something and then let our thoughts run along the line of, "I don't see how it can happen" or, "It probably won't happen", we're denying it; we're sabotaging our affirmation.

Always, that to which we give our attention will come to pass. If we think and believe in limitation we experience limitation because that's what we've given our attention to. Similarly, if we've the consciousness of prosperity we attract and experience prosperity. Remember the Golden Rule of Truth: 'whatever you have in consciousness, more of the same will be given! '

The certainty of belief

None of us doubts that the sun will rise each morning – we just know with complete certainty that it'll happen. We believe with complete certainty that when we're called to dinner that there'll be food on the table. Likewise we believe with complete certainty that when we push a button in the elevator for the fifth floor that we'll be taken to the fifth floor. This is the same type of expectancy we must have in our believing.

It isn't the thought of or by itself that causes things to change. When that wise person said that thoughts become things he forgot to mention the addition of one important ingredient for this to become true -- emotion, feeling, conviction, belief. Perhaps the adage ought to be, 'thoughts believed in are things', or 'thoughts become the things we believe'.

When all is said and done, the meaning of life, the surest way to achieve our goals and to receive the fulfilment of our dreams, can be boiled down to one simple word – **BELIEF**.

The importance of belief cannot be stressed enough. Upon this one idea our whole future, happiness and security lies because if what we believe is the foundation upon which our lives rest, then we can change our lives by changing our beliefs. Although it sounds simple it is the 'doing' that seems difficult because if we believe something is difficult, then for us it will be.

Thought and belief in a nutshell

Mind is the arena where thought takes place. No one can do our thinking for us and so we have complete control over what we choose to think. It's almost like having a field in which to sow anything we want except, instead of sowing plants, we sow thoughts. The beautiful thing about the mind is that we can sow thoughts in it at any time -- day or night, summer or winter -- and these thoughts can be of any variety that we choose -- positive or negative, giving or forgiving.

We need to understand that to take charge of our lives we have to take charge of our thoughts. This includes controlling the idle chatter that seems to continually go on in our mind and the conversations that we have with ourselves. We need to train our thoughts, to guide them so that our habitual thoughts are always positive and become a way of life. Whatever we hold in mind is what will manifest; thoughts of peace and prosperity will express themselves in positive and loving ways while thoughts of success and confidence will likewise manifest. It's always our thoughts and beliefs which create our experiences.

If we've been successful in changing and controlling our thinking and believe that a greater good is possible, we may be tempted to rest on our laurels and to assume that is all there is. WRONG!

Certainly things will improve. Life may seem happier and we may feel more content. But, instead of having to battle each problem individually, wouldn't it be better to deal with everything at once? Wouldn't it be preferable to be able to say, "Abracadabra" and to then find that it's done?

Read on, things are beginning to get exciting.

A SIMPLE EXPLANATION OF BELIEF

Although much has been written on the subject of belief, many of us feel it's an elusive something which very few can ever experience.

Belief is, in fact, an invisible trigger or impulse which activates a process much like getting into an elevator. Although the elevator has the power to go to any floor in a building, only we can activate that power by pushing a button to choose a floor.

Without giving it a second thought we just believe that when we push a particular button that the elevator will take us to that floor. We don't stand at the elevator door wondering how it will get us there. If we choose the third floor, for example, we don't question whether or not it'll take us to that floor or whether it'll take us to another floor instead!

We can see the parallel in our own lives. Life is, in fact, like a three step process:

1. We make a choice -- we use our mind to decide which floor we want to go to (i.e. we decide what it is that we want to experience in life).

2. We believe the elevator will get us there (i.e. we have faith and trust in the right outcome of our choice).

3. The elevator accomplishes its mission without any help from us. In other words we let go and attract that which we expect – that which is in our consciousness.

POINTS TO REFLECT UPON

1. There is one fundamental rule/law in life: **WHATEVER WE BELIEVE IS WHAT WE'LL EXPERIENCE.**

    This means that if we believe we are sick or in lack, then we shall possibly remain sick and continue to experience lack. If we're in love and have that exalted feeling that the birds are singing, the trees and flowers are smiling and that everything is happy and wonderful, then we shall be happy and carefree for as long as we maintain that feeling.

2. What do you believe? For each of us the important thing is to be continually aware of our thinking. Belief is the key! Again and again it must be stressed that, "It is done unto you as you believe".

    The person who believes that they 'have' will 'have'. It's all a matter of consciousness. Believing that we 'have' sets up an aura of attraction around us.

3. **"It's done unto us as we believe,"** can be said in so many different ways:

    - our lives reflect what we're thinking and believing,
    - what we give out (consciously or subconsciously) is a reflection of our inner thoughts and beliefs,
    - what we do speaks louder than what we say,
    - what counts is what goes on in our mind; it's NOT what we say,
    - it's as we think because this sets up waves (vibrations) which attract similar waves,
    - it's the beliefs that we have, surrounded by emotion and feeling, that drive us – it isn't just our thoughts by themselves.

4. **Some more gems.**

- No one can do our thinking for us.

- Trying to do one thing, while believing that another thing is
true is like trying to get east while driving west!

- Our thought is the director of our action.

- If we take the 'c' out of reaction and put it in front we'll find
that's what's happening to our reaction -- it is creating
according to our thought and belief!

Chapter 3

CONNECTING WITH THE POWER OF THE UNIVERSE

" And ye shall know the truth,
and the truth shall make you free.."
(John 8:32)

We've all heard the exhortations; some we've even mouthed ourselves:

"Just believe!"
"You need more faith."
"Think more positively."
"Don't be so negative."
"Let go and let God."
"The universe will take care of it."

And how often, when things don't go as planned, have we chastised ourselves or had criticisms such as, "Well you didn't believe enough", thrown at us?

It's all very well to say we believe, or that we must have belief, or that belief needs to be added to thought, but what is it we should believe in? Is it our own human will power, a force outside of us, or something else altogether?

If nothing happens by chance then logic dictates that everything happens because of something. That something is our consciousness – the sum total of our conscious and subconscious thoughts, feelings and beliefs. And right here many people eagerly ask, "How do I use this to my advantage to achieve what I really want to experience in life?"

It's a very relevant question and in this and the following chapters we look at how we can connect with and use the power of the universe.

So what is belief?

In essence, belief is energy, an invisible power that acts upon our thoughts thereby making them so real that we have no doubt. Like thought, belief is an activity controlled by us alone and by no one else. The importance of belief in shaping our lives cannot be stressed enough.

To believe in something our human mind usually follows one of two courses of action.

1. One way involves an individual believing that they alone are the controlling force that makes things happen.

    This type of person frequently tells themself that if they just had enough will power they could accomplish their desires or, if they just tried hard enough, work hard enough, believe in themself enough, then they'd achieve whatever they wanted to achieve. Whether they realise it or not, these people are saying that they're the ones doing the creating; they're using will power to try to make something happen.

    Although will power is beneficial in some cases, it has four drawbacks:

    - It's exhausting, both mentally and physically (the person using will power has to provide all the energy).

    - When the will power stops, so does the achieving.

    - The action is usually aimed at one thing at a time (health, prosperity, love, etc.)

    - The whole concept of will power is based on 'getting' something. It follows that anyone who thinks that they need to 'get' believes that they don't 'have'.

2. The second course of action is by a person who understands that there's a universal energy they're using when they think and that it's this universal energy that's responsible for the 'doing'. Instead of believing that their individual mind is the

controller, this person believes that their words of faith are acted upon by some kind of power that somehow brings about a desired result.

Many people have been confused at this point for the simple reason that they've failed to fully understand the true nature and operation of such a power. But let's get back to basics for a minute.

Separation - v – unity

There are at least three main ways in which we can look at life.

1. We can believe that each of us is an isolated being, living day-to-day as best as we can. At times this almost feels like being a cork in the ocean bobbing around aimlessly, making the best of circumstances as they unfold, and that each person is responsible to and for themselves alone.

2. A second way of looking at life is to believe that our lives are dependent upon and controlled by some external power, as taught by some religions.

3. The third way is a belief in a limitless, all-encompassing power or energy which is as much a part of us as we are of It ('It' is capitalised when the reference is to the Law, as in the Law of Life or Law of Cause and Effect). This isn't an external power, but one that is both internal and infinite.

The first two ways could be regarded as living in a state of separation while the third is what some call a state of Oneness.

Separation

The line of thought that there is a power external to us is often depicted in Michelangelo-type works of art. Such a power may be interpreted as a god-made-in-man's-image and is frequently regarded as something 'up' or 'out' there that must be pleaded or bartered with – "Please, I promise to be good if you'll just do this one more thing for me!"

This suggests a type of capricious power (or god) which might at times act on our behalf. To further compound the problem with this type of power is that some believe and are taught that they don't have direct access to this power and so must go through an intermediary who has some type of special relationship with it, thus permitting them to intervene on behalf of another. Belief in this type of a power involves a separation, not being one with it.

Unity or Oneness

Another line of thought is that there is only one infinite power or Law that not only operates in and through everything but is Itself the totality of everything. In this type of scenario each individual life form is an expression of this power and expresses at the individual's level of understanding. Consequently there is no separation, only Oneness with all that is, has been, or can be.

In this Oneness, the idea of 'having' is paramount since nothing could be separate from that Oneness. Therefore, the revelation of this power is through an understanding of 'having', as opposed to an attitude of 'getting'. And since the individual is One with the Whole, they are not creating, but co-creating, through their thoughts and actions.

If the nature of this power is separateness, or separation, then we as individuals play no part in the direction of our lives. If, on the other hand, the nature of this power is Oneness and unity, then we have the means to create our heart's desire since we are using an infinite and unlimited power every time we think or act.

We'll come back to this line of thought shortly but let us now go back to the quotation at the top of this Chapter, "Ye shall know Truth and the Truth will set you free."

What is meant by the "Truth"* and how does it set us free? (* The "T" of the word "Truth" is capitalised when referring to Law.)

If everything is in our life because we have attracted it through our thoughts, feelings and emotions, the question is, "How does this happen?" And when we consider the quotation at the beginning of

22

this Chapter we might also ask, "What is the Truth," and "How will it set us free?"

It's all very well to say that all we have to do is to control our thinking, to believe and to think positively, but how does that create things for us?

Central to the fact that nothing happens by chance is the understanding that it's our state of mind (i.e. our consciousness, the types of believing thoughts that we have) that affects us; it's our state of mind that radiates or sends out vibrations which attract similar types of vibrations. It's the old principle of magnetism: like attracts like. We too have a field around us that is continually attracting things that are similar to our state of mind (our consciousness).

Understanding this Chapter's quotation hinges on the word 'know'. There are two directives in the order, "Know the Truth", which must be equally applied if we are to achieve anything:

(i)   to 'know' in the sense that we are to have the knowledge and understanding (i.e. the intellect) of what is meant by Truth, and

(ii)   to 'know' in that we are to accept and embody (i.e. to understand intuitively) to such a degree that it is so much a part of our consciousness that we give no thought to it.

We see therefore that to, "Know the Truth", means to not only understand it intellectually but to personify it within our being to such a degree that we live it without thinking about it as something separate from us. It's much like breathing. We all know we breathe but very few of us spend each moment concentrating on the mechanisms involved because we have embodied the process and don't give it a second thought.

So when we asked earlier, "What should we believe in?", the answer is, "The Truth". But what is this Truth? Simply, that there is an infinite, limitless power or energy which is always working through the Law of Cause and Effect.

It's that same energy, or Strong Nuclear Force that holds neutrons and protons together in the nucleus of an atom and is causing the universe to expand at ever increasing speeds. This energy has no volition – it can't choose, it just acts. At the human level this energy, or life force, acts upon our beliefs and emotions to produce an exact replica in our external world.

In other words, we choose and It delivers! What could be simpler?

It doesn't matter what we call this power. Through-out recorded time it's been given so many different names and since It is unlimited there's an unlimited number of names we can give it: Life, the life force, Mother Earth, universal energy, the great I Am, universal awareness, infinite intelligence, divine mind, creative energy, infinite spirit, the great infinite, the great power, God, Father, and even "It". Such names merely refer to a principle that is eternally in operation, regardless of whether we know, understand, or believe it.

It's been called the great Law or Principle of Life which is the term I prefer to use. And just like physical laws such as gravity, mathematics, and electricity, It can't be seen but is always present, just waiting for us to plug into it through our thoughts. It's something we're always using either consciously or unconsciously and It's purely reactive -- It has no volition and so can't choose to work sometimes and not at other times.

Simply put, our experiences in life are the result of the way we use the Law of Life. Passionately and earnestly believed thoughts always manifest!

When we know this we can consciously direct this energy to produce what we want rather than what we don't want. And so the Truth (as in, "Ye shall know the Truth and the Truth shall make you free") may be summed up in just five words:

THERE IS ONLY ONE POWER

(Or, alternatively, THERE IS ONLY ONE UNIVERSAL ENERGY OR LIFE-FORCE).

Some people believe that the so-called 'fall of man' occurred when we moved from a belief in Oneness to a belief in separation. This was when mankind made a god-in-his-own-image; one to whom many pray begging that their needs be filled.

Knowing and understanding the Truth about this universal power or life force is the crux of the statement that THERE IS ONLY ONE POWER. It's the application of this knowledge that sets us free.

Moving from Separation to Unity

For too long mankind has lived in awe of a super-being dwelling 'out there' or 'up in the sky'. Artists and some religions describe 'him' as a being with a long flowing beard presiding in a place called heaven where some of us go to after a thing called death. The rest of humanity, according to that theory, go to another place, called hell, ruled by an arch enemy of god called the devil.

It is easy to see how such stories arose. The written word, as we know it, has only been in existence for a short period of time and the printing press is a relatively recent phenomenon. Stories were previously passed down from generation-to-generation through the spoken word.

People looked at appearances and made judgements about them. They thought they saw scarcity and developed a belief in lack. They saw the power of nature and judged it as something apart from themselves. They saw men doing 'evil' things and imagined and blamed a power they called the devil. These beliefs have been repeated generation after generation creating what we now refer to as race belief or race consciousness.

Today, most people realise that much of race belief is based on misinterpretation by our five senses. Quantum physics shows us that the observed is influenced by the observer. Science is also showing us that all material things are made up of the same atomic parts – thereby demonstrating a unity in the universe. We are moving toward an acceptance of the Truth of Oneness. Our growth as individuals is dependent on our commitment to work on our minds and to understand and 'know' the Truth, and to not give our power to a separate entity.

Getting in the flow

Just as electricity is forever flowing and is activated by the flick of a switch, we too can turn the switch on in our mind by thinking according to the nature of Oneness -- love, peace, joy, abundance and all good. And when we concentrate on Oneness we see and experience its effects -- prosperity, health, financial supply, enjoyable work, etc.

Our whole objective is to clear up our own mind, to knock down the barriers of separation (fear, hate, anger, lack and limitation) and in its place to see Oneness.

There is only one way to connect with this infinite and creative energy and that is through our thoughts and beliefs! There is only one way to shape our individual lives and that is through consciously directing our thoughts.

There are numerous ways of doing this but affirmations and affirmative prayer (also known as spiritual mind treatment) are the most powerful. These are specific ways of thinking and getting connected to the power and in the next chapter we'll learn how to do this.

When we understand that the universe is pure energy and that we're immersed in and one with universal energy, we can experience it by focussing our thoughts on what we want, NOT on what we don't want.

We are assured of success when we realise that this power can only reflect our thoughts and desires because there is no opposition in Oneness. We see, then, that to live successfully and to get the results we want in our lives, our role is to:

- focus our attention on what we do want, not on what we don't want,

- believe that we are always immersed in and one with a universal energy or life force that is forever present and able to fulfil our desire by becoming the manifestation of that desire, and

- be grateful and to act as though the desired end results were already accomplished.

We grow in consciousness through constructive practices such as affirmations and affirmative treatments. Let's move on, then, to explore exactly how to do this.

POINTS TO REFLECT UPON

1. We need to understand that the Truth that sets us free is the embodiment of the idea that THERE IS ONLY ONE POWER and that this universal energy, or life force, is present in its entirety in all places at all times. Like all forms of energy it's non-volitional and so acts according to the direction given to it by our believing words and thoughts to produce their physical counterpart.

2. Truth is the knowledge, understanding and acceptance that the universal energy and presence that is, **IS**.

    Knowledge refers to the fact that there is only one universal Law which is also known as the Law of Cause and Effect, or the Law of Life.

    Understanding means the comprehension that It is flowing in, through, around, over and under as everything all the time; that All of It constitutes the physical world in which we live, move and have our being.

    Acceptance is the knowledge that our word directs this unlimited energy.

3. Our thought is our individual use of this universal energy. When we know this we choose words and thoughts that are constructive. We don't plead or beg because there is no power external to us that can fulfil our desires. Nothing happens by chance! EVERYTHING is a perfect reflection of our beliefs, feelings and expectations.

4. We already know how to use the laws of electricity and gravity but, until we learn how to constructively use the Law of Life, we won't achieve our heart's desire. An intellectual understanding is not enough; nothing will happen until we consciously apply the Truth. Again – NOTHING HAPPENS BY CHANCE.

5. To create and experience greater good we need to:

   - continually nurture an "I have" feeling about our desires knowing that it's our beliefs that create and,

   - understand that we don't accomplish results by the power of our thought (i.e. will power), but through our deliberately directed words and thoughts since the Law of Cause and Effect will cause the thing thought of, and believed in, to appear.

6. The great truism of life is that: **IT IS DONE UNTO YOU AS YOU BELIEVE**.

Chapter 4

GOING WITH THE FLOW

"My words fly up, my thoughts remain below;
Words without thoughts never to heaven go."
(Hamlet; Act III, scene III)

Now that we know that nothing happens by chance, that everything is the result of how we use the Law of Life, we can use this knowledge to make the changes we want to see in our lives.

The first Law of Thermodynamics states that energy can be transferred (changed from one form into another) but it can never be created or destroyed. Accordingly, we can rely on and confidently use universal energy knowing that it changes form according to the direction we give it through our belief system.

The movement of our thought from an intellectual understanding of this energy to an intuitive and all-encompassing embodiment of It is how we consciously connect with It. We use It by speaking and thinking constructively or affirmatively.

Various terms are used to describe this process, the most common being:

- Affirmations,
- Directed, creative or affirmative thought,
- Affirmative prayer (spiritual mind treatment).

From this point on, the term '**affirmative thinking**' is used to cover all these expressions.

Basically, there are two formats of affirmative thinking and both are expanded upon in this Chapter:

- **affirmations** which are short, precise and positive statements, and

- **affirmative prayer (spiritual mind treatment)** which is a process used to consciously align our thoughts to the Truth of any given situation.

At any point in time our thinking is either focused and is directing our deliberately chosen words or thoughts in a specific direction, or it's unfocused, thereby leaving us like corks in the ocean -- bobbing first one way, then another, according to race belief.

Logic shows, therefore, that both focussed and unfocussed thinking form our affirmations. To experience life's riches our task is to work on maintaining a habitual attitude of positive, affirmative thinking.

Many people say affirmations in the belief that their words will affect or cause a power 'up' or 'out' there to somehow respond favourably to them. Others believe that a continual repetition of an affirmation will force something to happen. In actual fact affirmative thinking serves one purpose only -- to CONFIRM (to make firm) within our own mind that what we're saying is true and already is!

We've been shown that there is only one power and that It's present everywhere at all times. We're always using It either consciously or unconsciously and It faithfully creates according to our believing words and thoughts. That's what the Law of Attraction is all about – attracting results which perfectly correspond to our thinking and beliefs.

Affirmative thinking is to bring both our spoken words and the quiet chit-chat of our inner mind into alignment with the truth of what we're saying; it's to convince ourselves of the truth of what we're affirming! It's not just a matter of saying, "I am prosperous", hoping that someone or something will make us prosperous! No! We say it and accept it as a fact with all our being and belief and then the Law of Life has no option but to manifest by attracting results comparable to our consciousness.

This process is not new. For thousands of years we've been told, "It is done unto you as you believe."

Individual life, therefore, is a statement of what each person believes as true for themself. The thoughts and ideas that we believe will be returned to us in a way that is equal to our belief or conviction just as a mirror reflects an image back at the viewer.

For example, the statement, "I have no money", is an affirmation claiming lack and will be returned in the form of a dwindling bank account or being passed over for a raise at work. Happily the opposite is true and so the statement, "All is good; I'm always loved and absolutely cared for", if truly accepted, will boomerang back to us with happy feelings, loving relationships, and acts of appreciation.

Mental equivalents

What we've been talking about are 'mental equivalents'. And since the Law of Life is that we can only attract that which is equal to what is in our consciousness, the key is to build mental equivalents of what we do want and to rid ourselves of the mental equivalent of the things we don't want.

This means changing our habitual thoughts and building new mental equivalents filled with the feelings of joy and excitement that we experience when our desires are fully met. If we don't possess enough of some particular thing we desire, our mental equivalent of that thing has been diminished and we need to work on enlarging it through affirmative thinking.

One simple way to help increase our mental equivalents is to be grateful for every sign of good that appears; it has a seemingly miraculous multiplier effect. Gratitude for friends and family attracts and multiplies more love and harmony in our lives; prosperity is increased when we are grateful for what we have; and our health blossoms when we continually give thanks for a perfectly functioning body.

When we build a mental equivalent of something, we're creating a consciousness for it and yes .... consciousness always manifests!

Much to my chagrin I've experienced the workings of this Law on a number of occasions when the result was not what I wanted. For example I once held a senior management position which I thoroughly detested. One of the reasons was that although I had the title of 'Executive Director' I had no decision-making power. I started looking for another position and built up a mental picture of leaving – in other words I created a mental equivalent of not being in that position. Unfortunately (for my wallet) I was abruptly fired before I had found a replacement job.

This taught me the importance of building a mental equivalent of what I do want, not of what I don't want. In this case, instead of seeing myself getting out of what I felt was a no-win situation, I should have been building a mental equivalent of being firmly established in a secure position where I was happy, appreciated for my abilities and talents, had a good working relationship with fellow employees, and was marvellously remunerated.

Similarly, a friend used to complain bitterly about having to get up to go to work early each day. One day she was laid off and it took her six months to find another job. She never again complained about having to get up early!

Both of these stories illustrate that the Law always manifests according to our mental equivalents.

To build a new mental equivalent we need to visualise or mentally see ourselves doing the things we want to do and experience. We need to truly feel the emotions that go along with our desires and to imagine ourselves actually living in the new mental equivalent. At first it may feel phoney but with practice it becomes easier and then, without fanfare, the day arrives when the mental equivalent manifests.

The purpose and the process of affirmative thinking

The purpose of affirmative thinking is to align our consciousness with the good we want to experience. This re-alignment sinks into our subconscious mind as habitual thought patterns which are the cause of our experiences.

The prime purpose of life is to demonstrate as much good, and love, and peace, and health, and prosperity, that we can embody. Affirmative thinking is not to get something but to acknowledge and accept that something already is although it may, to our physical senses, still be in the invisible.

Whenever we consciously use affirmative thinking we must use words that show we believe we already have the desired end result. If we think in terms of what is generally referred to as 'negative' thoughts of fear, doubt, anger or lack, then that's what we're affirming. But when our words and thoughts are filled with 'positive' emotions (e.g. love, peace, harmony, health, abundance) then that's what we're affirming and we'll attract their equivalent in greater quantity.

Simply stated, repetitive thoughts become affirmations which are acted upon by universal energy to produce equivalent results. The process works the same for everyone, all the time. To sum up:

1. We focus our attention **on what we want to experience.**

2.   We take our attention **away from what we don't want to experience** (remember the three monkeys: see no evil, hear no evil and speak no evil).

3. We tell ourselves that there are **no obstructions** to our good; that **there are no limitations**; that all barriers to our good have ceased to exist.

4. We see the good we desire by feeling it, speaking it, believing it and giving thanks that it has manifested itself in the visible **NOW!**

Affirmations

The most effective affirmations use actions words that stir up an emotional experience. For example, "I'm as joyously enthusiastic as a jubilant and over-active five-year old" has more emotional impact than "I'm happy". So it's important to use 'feeling' language.

When composing an affirmation remember to use the four Ps' -- **personal** (I am ....), **positive** (I am joyously enthusiastic), **present** (NOW, not tomorrow, or next month, or next year, but NOW!), and **precise** (the shorter and more to the point an affirmation is, the more power it has).

We need also to be specific. If it's a four bedroom house overlooking the ocean that you're affirming, then affirm that; don't just affirm a house. Be careful, though, not to outline. We can't say that it has to be a specific house because it may belong to someone else, or it may have a structural problem. You might get that house but then find out too late that there's something wrong with it.

In this situation, an effective affirmation would be along the lines of, "I now joyously claim ownership of my own fantastic four-bedroom dream home overlooking the ocean. It's the right home for me, fully paid for and secure in every detail. I'm so ecstatic and grateful for my perfect right home in the perfect and right environment."

Affirmative prayer (Spiritual Mind Treatment)

Many New Thought teachings use a 4, 5 or 6-step process called affirmative prayer or Spiritual Mind Treatment. The basic steps are as follows:

1. Purpose. Every affirmative prayer/treatment must have a definite purpose. Like affirmations, just saying we'd like more money, or to feel happier, is not sufficient. We must be as specific as possible without outlining how something should be done. For example, "This treatment is for the greater realisation of peace and harmony at home ", or "This

affirmative prayer is for increased clarity in my decision-making process at work."

2. Recognition. This step involves recognising such points as, "There is only one infinite intelligence (or life force) that's present in all places at all times as peace, wisdom, harmony, and joy. It's creative. It's the energy of the universe forever moving in and out of form. It's all good!"

3. Unification. This step, also known as identification, builds on the first step.

   After recognising that there is only one energy (life force or infinite power and presence) we identify ourselves with It. This is where we affirm that we are IN and OF the ONE, that we have all of Its qualities in potential and that our individual "I am" is our personal use of the great "I AM". We vividly acknowledge our oneness with the creative energy of the universe.

4. Realisation. Having recognised and consciously united our mind with the ONE we enter into a state of realisation that whatever it is we choose to experience is already here in potential. We speak our word with the conviction that our believing thought and word is the power that stirs invincible law into action (i.e. makes things happen). Without such a deep trust and belief our spoken words are just that -- spoken words, and accomplish nothing.

5. Thanksgiving -- gratitude confirms our beliefs. Remember, gratitude is the greatest causal energy in the universe.

6. Release. This is an important but frequently overlooked step. If we affirm something but then continue to worry about whether-or-not or how our affirmations and treatments are being answered, we're like a gardener who digs up a bulb to see if it has taken root. We know that if we did that then the bulb would never grow since it's not being left to mature at its own rate in its own time.

We must 'let go' knowing that the Law of Life is always working. It would be beneficial to affirm something like, "I have activated the Law and I am at peace, content to wait for the fulfilment of my heart's desire." Remember – fear and anxiety are an indication of a lack of belief.

After speaking words of release we rest in the knowledge that the right lead now presents itself. Somewhere, somehow, we will read, hear or think something that will jump out at us and we'll have an inkling of what we're to do next.

There's an old saying, "Treat and move your feet". We can't afford to be like the man who, when told that God was the source of all his good and would take care of all his needs, went and quit his job, didn't pay his bills and when the bailiff came to evict him said, "But God is going to take care of me."

Nor should we be like the lady who believed a psychic who told her that she was going to win a lottery. She gave away her home and furniture and got ready to travel because that's what she wanted to do with her 'winnings'. Ten years later she was still waiting for her windfall – in rented accommodation.

In these cases the people concerned put their belief in another person, or in what the other person told them. Their belief wasn't in the power within and so was not built on a firm foundation.

Why do affirmations sometimes seem not to work?

If it looks as though our affirmations or affirmative prayers and treatments aren't working it doesn't help to be told, "Ye have asked amiss", or to be told that our belief wasn't strong enough.

We need to remember that our affirmative thinking always demonstrates when our consciousness crosses the 51% threshold of embodying the mental equivalent. We're all good at choosing what we'd like to experience but believing, beyond all doubt that it's ours, may prove a bit more difficult at times.

Certainly we shouldn't blame ourselves or get angry or upset if things don't appear to be working immediately; the Law of Life will only attract more anger or things to be upset about. Instead, we're to go back to our feeling nature and re-build the mental equivalent of what we do want, not what we don't want!

One word sums all this up – **PRACTICE**! And then more practice! And then even more practice!

Practice means taking charge of our thoughts, of being in control of our own destiny.

A final word

Before we leave this exploration of affirmative thinking let's again look at the last step of affirmative prayer.

Every affirmation must include the idea of completion, of fulfilment right now. We need to move away from the notion that the demonstration will come in the future; we need to enter into a frame-of-mind which knows only the here and now, one which knows only completion right at this moment.

We should leave each affirmative prayer or treatment with a feeling of joyful expectancy, just as a child feels such great happiness at Christmas time when he or she knows beyond all doubt that Father Christmas has brought them what they asked for.

We should leave each treatment with the feeling of completion affirming, "It is done." We must know that nothing is too good to be true, that nothing is too wonderful to happen, and that nothing is too good to last.

POINTS TO REFLECT UPON

1. We are immersed in an infinite creative medium (universal energy or creative law) which creates after the pattern that our thought gives It. This means that our lives are a reflection of the mental equivalent we hold in consciousness.

2. When we understand that life is a process and that it involves our personal use of a universal Principle which is as simple to use as turning on a vacuum cleaner or flipping a light switch, we understand that our every thought is an affirmation.

3. Like a boomerang or a reflection in a mirror, whatever we give out will be returned to us with the exact same level of intensity. Thoughts and feelings of doubt, fear or lack are a form of affirmative thinking and we can be sure that these affirmations will be answered with more doubt, fear and lack. Fortunately, thoughts of love, peace, harmony and faith will also be returned in equal measure.

4. In any discussion on affirmative thinking we must remember that:

    - affirmations are not ways of attempting to get something; they are ways of confirming in our mind that we already 'have' because of our relationship with the Law which governs all life, and

    - our believing thoughts become our habitual prayer.

    We need to become more aware of our thoughts (be like a gardener); we must continually be on guard and act as though we 'have' as opposed to trying to 'get'.

5. Affirmative thinking does something to us – not to anyone else -- and is answered according to our belief. The two ingredients of feeling and belief must be present for directed affirmations to out-picture otherwise we're likely to say they aren't answered.

Chapter 5

PROVE ME NOW

"... prove me now herewith, saith the Lord of Hosts, if I will not open you the windows of heaven and pour you out a blessing, that there shall not be room enough to receive it."
(Malachi 3:10).

Nothing happens by chance; everything happens according to the way we use the Law of Life (the Law of Cause and Effect). The people and situations in our life are always the consequence of the way we've used our mind. Consciousness is cause and we learned in the previous chapter how to change our consciousness through affirmative thinking.

Whether or not the results in our lives match our desires, the truth is that we're proving the Law all the time. Whatever we believe is what we experience in the outer. It's not the words we say or the things we do that drive the Law of Life, but what's going on inside of us – our beliefs, feelings and emotions.

This means we could be saying one thing ("I claim financial abundance", for example) but expressing another (perhaps financial lack) because we've been thinking such things as, "I hope it appears", or, "I wonder if it'll happen?" The Law of Life works on the feelings and convictions we have inside of us, not on the words we speak in the outer.

Law always produces but in this particular example it's been used in reverse and produced negative results instead of the verbal positive desire. We need to understand that it's just thought used the wrong way that produces the results we don't really want.

As one wise person once said, "There is no sin but a mistake and no punishment but the consequences of that mistake." But now we're learning the correct way to use thought and through affirmative thinking we use it to bring improved health, increased prosperity, more love and new forms of creative self-expression into our personal experience.

The purpose of life is to decide what we want and to let it happen by believing that a limitless power, acting upon our believing thoughts and words, always produces according to the direction we give it. Could anything be simpler or more straightforward? This is the secret that sets us free from unwanted experiences!

Doing Our Part

Our job is to prove to ourselves that this is the way the Universe works. We don't need to convince anyone else that consciousness is what really causes things to happen. Our responsibility is to ourselves, to become vitally alive, to radiate the Truth in all we think, do and say. Our part in all of this is to believe and to then accept the results of our beliefs. Since all is Law we always receive what we put out – failure if we doubt, success if we believe.

We understand that no one can do this for us; that each of us, alone in the quiet of our inner self, can accept the freedom that results from living the Truth. We come to realise that we're in the express business -- always expressing the perfect results of our individual use of the Law. And like a strong magnet we attract the people, opportunities and prosperity that are in alignment with our beliefs.

Since we know that we attract everything that's in accord with our consciousness we make sure that our consciousness reflects only that which we want to experience. Gradually we understand that our job is to lower the barriers in our mentality, to unlock the doors of resistance, to knock down the walls of, "I can't", "It's too good to be true", "I'm not worthy", "I'm not ready", etc.

Proving that good is pouring into our lives is a very personal thing; we must convince ourselves that our consciousness causes things to happen. The same thing could be experienced by two different people and one would call it a blessing while the other might call it a curse. Who is right? They both are! One is happy with the blessing; the other is angry or sad with the curse.

So why do they experience feelings totally opposite from each other if they experience the same result? It's because their interpretations, based on their belief systems, are total opposites. Our interpretations of whether we are proving the Law or proving that things happen randomly is, ultimately, a personal choice.

But we don't have to fool ourselves into believing we are proving that the Law works or that our consciousness is the cause. As it says in Matthew 7:20, "... by their fruits, ye shall know them." So let's ask ourselves, "What fruits am I producing in my life? What experiences am I experiencing? What do I know about myself based on what's going on in my life at the moment?" When we look at it this way we'll then know what we are subconsciously or habitually thinking and believing.

If we wish to prove the Law, here are some suggestions for affirmation prayer/treatment for what is known as the Square of Life.

The square of life

The term, 'the square of life', refers to the four main areas of life which combine to provide fulfilment: health, prosperity, love and self-expression.

Using the affirmative prayer/treatment process outlined in the previous chapter, the following are examples of the types of words we can use to train ourselves to think affirmatively to shape our consciousness and attract greater good through the invincible Law of Life.

It's important, however, that we individualise our affirmations by choosing words that we understand and feel comfortable with -- remember, we're not talking to anything outside of ourselves; we're talking to our own inner self! The more spontaneous the affirmations and the greater the belief that they will be fulfilled by Law, then the more certain the result will be.

1. SELF EXPRESSION

Perhaps it's a new or better position that we're looking for. In that case we speak words similar to the following with as much conviction, feeling and visualisation as possible:

(i)   "There is only one life force, one power, one presence. This life force is the infinite expression of the universe flowing in and through all things at all times. It's peace, harmony, love, power, wisdom and all good."

(ii)   "This life force animates and sustains me. I'm one with it and so, unified with this universal power and wisdom, I'm empowered to speak my word with complete confidence knowing that it's being fulfilled now!"

(iii)   "I claim the ideal position. It's the right position for me and it's available right now. I know that everyone and everything is working to unite me with this position. It meets all my requirements and expectations. It's well paid and my talents and strengths are used to the full. It's exciting and inspiring and I feel so comfortable. Working conditions and opportunities for growth and personal development are fantastic. There's only peace and harmony for everyone in the workplace. It's a healthy and happy place to work and I'm feeling so enthusiastic."

N.B. If the person speaking the affirmative prayer/treatment wants to change their current position, something along the following lines could be included at this point. "I let go my present position with a blessing for those who will take it. I know that these changes happen in the perfect way, at exactly the right time and with the right people. I affirm that everyone involved prospers."

(iv)   "I'm so grateful that my believing words are now being acted upon by the energy of the universe -- that life force that's always creating through me. I'm so grateful for my wonderful new, rewarding and creative position where I'm feeling so accepted and so happy."

(v)   "I now release my words into creative law in complete trust and confidence in the invincibility of the Law and I'm at peace experiencing a perfect outcome now."

2. PROSPERITY

The following are the types of affirmative statements that could be used for increasing financial supply:

(i)   "There is only one universal energy; One life; One Power; One intelligence; One substance. It's omnipresent, omnipotent, and omniscient."

(ii)   "I recognise that not only am I made in the image and likeness of this wonderful and very personal One but that It moves in, through, around and as me. I know there is a power, an energy, a vitality, a livingness flowing in and through me and out into everything I think, say, do or feel. I am the embodiment of this power, Its energy, Its vitality. I believe and fully trust in my unity with this power and presence."

(iii)   "I know that It is not only the source of my financial supply but is also the supply. I know that my believing word is law; that things are possible to me through this power which flows in and through me. I know that my believing thought is the thing itself in manifestation. Therefore all the good (or mention the specific form of prosperity that's being claimed) that I desire is manifest in my life right now through both expected and unexpected channels. It feels so good. I'm so happy and joyous as I feel the thrill of receiving my good. Prosperity, wealth, abundance, opulence are all mine now and I feel absolutely over the moon."

(iv)   "I'm so grateful for the abundant financial supply (or other form of good) that's appearing in my life in such amazing ways. I'm so thankful for the good that's manifesting for me now in such an amazing avalanche of prosperity and through so many seemingly miraculous channels."

(v)   "It is done. I let go knowing that the seed has been planted and that money and riches now sprout forth in my life. My garden is now blooming with an abundance of prosperity trees and flowers."

3. HEALTH

Likewise, we apply the same process for thoughts of perfect health until they become an integral part of our consciousness. When all the barriers and objections to perfect health are erased from our consciousness, improved health is experienced. We must know, think, feel, believe and see only perfect health; anything else is to believe in duality -- i.e. thinking about both good health and illness at the same time, thereby sabotaging our affirmations.

As an example, let's suppose you had an injured leg. Yes, it's very real in the physical and there are certain things you can do to assist in its healing – rest, physiotherapy, and general care. But, over and above this, the Law can be used to speed up and ensure a complete healing by visualising and affirming the perfectly functioning leg – affirm its flexibility, that you are freely running, jumping, swimming or whatever activity you would normally undertake with your perfectly functioning leg.

The goal is to see, feel and believe in the possibility of the end result we desire and in this case it's a perfectly healthy leg. We keep our attention on what we do want (a fully functioning, flexible and healthy leg). With conviction, we speak affirmative words such as:

(i)   "There is only one perfect life force flowing in and through me and all things. It's the essence of who I am. It knows only perfection; only wholeness; only perfect health. It's that which animates, maintains and sustains my physical body."

(ii)　　"Right now I attune myself to the realisation of my oneness with this energy, this life force which flows through me, automatically making everything whole. Every cell, every atom, every muscle, every nerve, every organ, every part of my physical being now radiates with wholeness and perfection."

(iii)　　"I know that this ever-present life force knows only wholeness and right now I feel It flowing through me renewing, revitalising and recharging every part of my body. I feel the surge of energy rushing through me. My legs are flexible, toned and nimble. I joyously walk, run, leap and swim easily and effortlessly. I feel it; I believe it. With every ounce of my being I accept this picture of total perfect health, of freedom of movement."

(iv)　　"I'm so grateful to know that I am perfect health; that I am whole, strong and physically perfect now and always. I'm just so grateful for the loving, healing presence always radiating through my life. I'm so grateful for perfect expression, for perfect health, for freedom of movement."

(v)　　"I release now move through life in joy, forever experiencing perfection in mind, body and soul."

4. RELATIONSHIPS / LOVE

Every day we interact with other people on a number of levels. Regardless of whether such contacts are at home, work or in a social setting, we need to know that we're always in the right place and with the right people.

The human part of us often cries out for love and recognition and at times we may feel that it has to come through a particular person. Too often we try to force a relationship because we're afraid of being alone. We try to convince ourselves that so-and-so is the 'right' person for us and we remain blind to signals which may be warnings of a potentially harmful or co-dependent relationship.

Our job is to affirm the right partner and a healthy, nurturing relationship for all concerned. In all our dealings with other people we could perhaps affirm that we're constantly with those who can help us and make us happy in a healthy and nurturing way and who, in turn, we can help and make happy.

An affirmative treatment for love, the right partner or the right relationship, might include the following elements:

(i)   An acknowledgement that there is only good. Remember, like attracts like so we start an affirmative treatment for the right relationship in the knowledge of Oneness and that it is all good. We claim the feeling and conviction that this is true.

(ii)   A specific definition of what it is we want to experience in life – e.g. a new partner, a more meaningful relationship, the ability to get on better with co-workers, etc.

(iii)   An emphasis on words and phrases such as 'the right partner', 'a nurturing relationship', 'happy', 'harmonious', 'trusting', 'honest', 'loving', 'caring', 'supportive', etc. We need to use such words with the conviction that they are right and true for us.

(iv)   An acceptance that the right person or relationship is seeking us, just as we're seeking them /it.

        Perhaps use statements such as, "I realise the nature of any relationship is love and I know I have a truly loving nature. The unity of Oneness insures that everyone and everything is in perfect and right relationship with everyone and everything else and I'm attracting the right person to me right now because of this."

        "The Law of Harmony only brings about my perfect harmonious relationship. I attract the Love that I am."

(v)   The knowledge and feeling that we're always being guided to the right place and the right person, and that we are always guided to say and do the right thing.

In conclusion

Throughout all such affirmative work we must maintain a continual awareness that we're using that ever-present life-force that surrounds and enfolds us. As many writers have stated, we must be alert, alive and awake to our good and have an inner burning realisation and acceptance of the right result.

We must embody the knowledge and feeling that there are no barriers to receiving our good and that the right outcome is now realised. We then give thanks that our desired good -- the right relationship, the new job, the increased financial supply, etc. has materialised in a perfect way and in perfect timing.

As an exercise, why not develop an affirmative statement for something you want to see realised in your life right now. Use the above points to develop an outline and change it daily if necessary, until there's a feeling that the essence of those words vibrate throughout your whole being. When that feeling is fully embodied, you'll be answered on the external.

POINTS TO REFLECT UPON

How do we prove that Law works?

1. Whether we like it or not, we're proving that Law works all the time, even when we're receiving what we don't want! That's because Law always takes our believing words and thoughts and reflects them into our life experience exactly as we have projected them -- just as a boomerang always returns, or as a mirror always reflects an image cast upon it.

2. If we're not experiencing what we say we want, we need to look at our beliefs associated with the desire – in other words, what's going on inside?

    Are we saying, "Yes", or are we saying, "I don't believe this", or "I hope it works", or "I wonder what's going to happen"? If we doubt, we're sabotaging our own affirmations and of course they won't manifest.

It's not what we want or wish that's important, it's how we think and feel inside (i.e. our beliefs and convictions) because that is what will externalise in our lives.

3. We need to understand that the Law of Life ALWAYS reacts to us. We need to achieve a consciousness which knows that this invincible power acts upon our believing thoughts and words by becoming that which we believe. Then we understand the importance of always consciously directing our thoughts.

4. Proof that the great Law of Life always works is summed up in the words from ancient scriptures, "By their fruits ye shall know them."

5. It's not the words we speak that tell the world of our relationship with the life-force forever flowing through us and maintaining us, but what happens to us. Our perfect "fruits" are expressions of perfect love, health, prosperity and self-expression. The not-so-perfect ones are the experiences of lack and limitation that we may occasionally experience.

Chapter 6

ABRACADABRA

(Albra Kedahbra -- Aramaic for "I will create as I speak".)

*"But seek ye first the kingdom and its righteousness, and all
these things shall be yours as well."*
(Matthew 6:33).

Most of us have at some time or other in our life wished we had a
magic wand, a lantern, an incantation such as "Abracadabra", or
some other tool that we could just wave or tap to have our every
desire fulfilled.

As a child I was enthralled with the story of Aladdin and his magic
lamp. How I wished I could have such a lamp, to be able to rub it
and to have a magic genie mysteriously rise up in a puff of smoke
to grant my every wish! The problem with that particular story was
that the genie would only grant three wishes but, as a child, I had it
all figured out. My first wish would be that I would have unlimited
wishes -- that way I would always have all my wishes granted.

How little I knew then that each of us does in fact have a magic
genie that grants our every wish. We call it by many names, the
most common being Life, energy, God, Infinite Mind, Universal
Intelligence, Spirit. And how little I realised that the magic wand I
so earnestly wished for was already an established fact -- my
believing word!

As I grew older, however, I thought less frequently of Aladdin and
more of how it was my responsibility to make things happen. And
by responsibility I mean my human responsibility, my human will
power and my blood, sweat and tears. Isn't that how race
consciousness says we succeed? Haven't we all fallen into that
trap?

As a child it's much easier to believe in a power greater than we
are, be it a genie, a magic wand, or a god. But as we get older we

think we have to do it all ourselves – either that or to let things happen by chance.

Occasionally we wish or dream of how wonderful it would be if the secret of life, or the path to successful living, could be neatly bundled into a simple exercise or statement that didn't require too much effort on our part. Some have even speculated that religion came into being because of man's innate laziness -- that by having an intermediary speaking or acting on our behalf we would be free to do whatever we wanted, whenever we wanted.

Whatever the truth may be, one thing is certain. Over countless centuries mankind's interpretation of the thing we call 'God' has moved from a belief in a process whereby we are of the same nature and so therefore create according to our desires, to an idea that we are separate from It and have no control over our lives. For many people this 'God' has become an external though invisible presence upon whom they call in times of need, beseeching and hoping against hope to receive an answer or sign.

Isn't it a relief to know the power is really within us, that the Law does the work, and that our only responsibility is to think correctly?

We grow in the realisation of who we really are as we come to understand, believe and accept that our word, which is a reflection of our thought, directs and distributes the ever-present universal energy within us. And as we grow in this realisation we understand more clearly that nothing happens by chance and that each of us has the ability to direct and control our lives as we choose; each of us can create a blueprint for personal success and fulfilment.

Let's get to it by splitting the quote at the beginning of this Chapter into three meaningful sections.

1.   First things first – "seek ye first the kingdom"

By aligning our thoughts and beliefs with what we call good (beauty, peace, love, harmony, abundance wisdom, freedom, joy, balance and order) the Law has no option but to reflect these qualities back to us as our experience.

The call to, "Seek ye first the kingdom", is a reminder to put first things first. First comes a consciousness of good, then the *experience of good na*turally follows. This is why the above quotation goes on to say, "Therefore do not be anxious about tomorrow, for tomorrow will be anxious for itself."

In the past our tendency may have been to turn to a god-made-in-the-image-of-man type of deity when we wanted something. Instead, our aim should be to understand that Law, or principle, is always working. It doesn't choose nor does It take holidays! Law always produces what It's asked to produce, just as mathematicians will always get '10' regardless of whether they add 5+5, or 2+8, or 1+9, or 4+6, or 3+7.

When we understand, truly understand, we'll see that we're always one with the Law, just as a drop of ocean water (which contains the same qualities as the entire ocean though obviously different in size) is always one with the entire ocean. When we understand 'Oneness', we know that whatever we ask for already exists albeit in another form.

We need to look no further than the weather to understand this process of changing form. When temperatures drop rain turns into ice, snow or sleet. Then as the temperatures increase, the ice, snow and sleet melt and turn into water. A further increase in temperature then causes steam, cloud and seemingly clear skies. It's all the same stuff appearing in different forms according to the temperature. So remember, our believing thoughts can change the form of the energy that we're immersed in to whatever form we have a mental equivalent of.

To ask for something is to affirm that we believe we don't have it and so we attract more of what we associate with the 'not having' of that thing. For example, if I'm asking for more income, it means I believe I don't have enough money and so I'm associating myself with not being able to do certain things like go on a trip or buy a new car. That association perpetuates my belief that I don't have enough! Remember -- to him who has in consciousness, more of the same will be given. How soon we forget!

By seeking first the 'kingdom' (as in the quote above) we're aligning ourselves with the Allness of what we earlier described as the multi-dimensional world where all is ONE. When we reside in this Oneness (in our mind, which is the only place where anything can happen) we are aware that we are an individual expression of the Whole, residing within the Whole, with the consciousness of the Whole. From this position of unity we grow in the understanding that we already 'have' (in Spirit), that we don't have to strive to 'get'.

Accordingly, our goal in life is to seek to dwell in the kingdom of Oneness which is that place where we live and continually know that we live in a state of peace, love, joy and harmony and where we experience only wholeness -- health, prosperity and wonderful self-expression. It's that place wherein our word is law and becomes the thing spoken or thought of because we know beyond all shadow of a doubt that we are One with that which is ALL.

This is what we earlier described as the Truth and we experience It by understanding, accepting, acknowledging and embodying the reality that THERE IS ONLY ONE perfect life-force always present. And this is where practice comes in. We need to practice thinking and realising that all the good we desire is here now; that it's not apart from us; that there isn't energy plus us, but only energy acting as us according to our choices.

Until we became aware that our consciousness made things happen we tried to fix effects with effects (e.g. fix a headache with aspirin or fix money troubles by borrowing more money). To put first things first, we start with cause -- we fix effects by changing cause.

2. Our sole (soul) responsibility –"and its righteousness"

To experience fulfilment at all levels of life we must look beyond appearances (i.e. that which we experience with our senses) to the Truth (i.e. Law always outpicturing). We think in terms of reality, instead of appearances.

This doesn't mean that we can think and believe in physical pain or ill health and at the same time expect the Law to take the pain away. Nor do we look at an empty wallet, believe in lack and expect the Law to fill our wallet with money. Our responsibility – and it's the only thing required of us – is to have the consciousness of health and prosperity. Then, and only then, can the Law go to work and show us how we can release the pain and fill our wallets.

It's like being an actor rehearsing for a new role. At first it feels awkward because we have to pretend while we're learning our lines but, once we start remembering them, we become more comfortable and we start to believe that we are the person we're portraying.

This is the same process we use for our affirmations – at first they may feel awkward but with practice we become more centred and assured of our words. And when that happens, wonderful things start to manifest on the external. So our job is to speak affirmative words of health, peace, harmony and prosperity and we're to act as though the words were true. But the, "Bringing it to pass", is the work of Law; it's not our job!

Each moment we have a choice in the way we think and act. We can consciously direct the Law or let race consciousness direct it for us. By directing our words and thoughts, and by believing and feeling with conviction that which we desire to experience in our lives, we prove the Truth. This is the essence of living an affirmative life.

When we do our affirmative treatments we are to believe that we have already received what we've asked for! The Law is working all the time regardless of our use of it ("its righteousness"). The 'kingdom' of "righteousness" is our correct thinking.

To get this firm in our minds let's go over the five main components of proving the Law.

(i)   <u>We understand who we are</u>.

Since each of us is one with the Law, we understand that we're all individualisations of the One. This means that each of us is in the express business -- always expressing at the level of our understanding of life.

(ii)   <u>We understand the working of the Law and that it's done unto us as we believe</u>.

We need to embody the idea that the Power and Presence that is, IS.

Remember -- whatever we have in consciousness, more of the same thing will be added! The Law is perfect. We need to know the Truth, to believe it, and to command it (through our spoken and believing word) to operate in our lives.

To **know** means to know that there is no obstruction, that nothing can hinder the operation of the Law of Cause and Effect, and that nothing in our consciousness can be withheld from us.

(iii)   <u>We accept that we've already received.</u>

We accept through affirming (i.e. MAKING FIRM) our belief. We get into the vibration of acceptance by speaking affirmations of Truth such as:

- "There is only One Power and Presence."

- "Since I'm one with It (made in Its image and likeness) I always have the power to change my experiences."

- "I speak my word and so direct the Law into right action."

-"I trust and let go knowing that right action is taking place in my life."

- "I give thanks knowing that I am receiving now."

-"I accept in the visible that which comes from the invisible."

There is only one way to achieve what we want to see manifest in our lives and that is to believe that we already have it, to act as though it were so. It is our believing words and thoughts that manifest!

(iv)   We stay in the vibration.

Too often we devote 10-20 minutes to meditation and affirmations in the morning and then go out into the world and join in with criticism, condemnation, negative thinking and discuss the 'awful things' of life. Suddenly we find that the peaceful thoughts that we'd experienced in meditation have suddenly flown out of the window!

Once we get into the vibration of Oneness we need to stay there 24/7 so that our habitual thoughts and words are words of love, peace, harmony and joy. Then, and only then, will we experience the bounty of life since we attract that which is in accord with our consciousness.

(v)   We're grateful.

An attitude of gratitude multiplies our good. Try it. Come up with a list of 20 things you're grateful for right now.

3.   Successful living and fulfilment – "and all these things shall be yours as well"

For me, one of the most thrilling and memorably experiences in life has been the understanding and realisation that we do not have to do anything, or force anything, or beg for anything to be done – and that includes begging a 'something' outside of us to do anything for us. The Truth is that it's already done! The Truth is that we already have!

The formula for successful living is laid out perfectly in the quote, *"Seek ye first the kingdom and its righteousness, and all these things shall be yours as well."*

We start with cause (our consciousness) and use it righteously. We use it to believe in the positive and so only good and joy and peace and love and prosperity and material 'things' will be ours through the working of the Law (*"these things shall be yours as well "*).

When we get this in the right order, we demonstrate easily and effortlessly.

POINTS TO REFLECT ON

1. It takes practice. We've learned that nothing happens by chance. This is a universe of cause and effect and our thoughts and beliefs (consciousness) are cause. When we align our consciousness with this Truth we move into a higher consciousness that brings unity and wholeness into our lives. We've learned that we can move into a higher consciousness by practicing affirmative thinking. As well, we know that we can prove to ourselves if It's working by being open and receptive and then looking at and interpreting the results.

2. As we practice directing our consciousness we may start with something like attracting a new job or new relationship. We start proving to ourselves that this works and in the process create a more believing consciousness which in turn makes our practice even more effective.

3. Ultimately we get to the point of not needing to do treatments for certain things, but to have our automatic, habitual thoughts trained to always seeing and experiencing good. That's the ultimate goal for each of us.

4. To live successfully we need to take control of our thinking. It's as simple as that! We need to train ourselves to turn from appearances and to centre our thinking on **what we do want** to see manifest in our lives, not to think or fret about what **we don't want**!

5. Since no one can do our thinking for us we need to continually be on guard, to be on fire with the belief that there is a universal energy, greater than we are individually, that is forever flowing through us taking the form of our belief.

6. All things are possible to the person who believes. That is the Law! We need to think of ourselves as the vehicle through which the Law operates. And just as a vehicle can't move without a driver, we use our mind to direct and move the limitless power that dwells within. In each of us it's that limitless life-force through which all things are possible. In fact, the only limit to what It can do is the limit we place on It in our mind.

Chapter 7

THE LAW OF LIFE

"Do not be conformed to this world but be transformed by the renewal of your mind, that you may prove what is ....good and acceptable and perfect".
(Romans 12:2)

In a nutshell

1. The Truth is simple to understand; it's the 'doing' that we're learning in this classroom called life. The measuring stick by which we can gauge our success is summed up in the oft repeated phrase, "By their fruits ye shall know them." In essence, the reality about life and our role in it is how we use the Law.

2. The Law of Life (aka the Law of Cause and Effect or the Law of Attraction) is that there is an infinite energy or life-force present in Its entirety everywhere in the universe at all times. It flows through us capturing our beliefs, feelings and convictions to produce the results in our lives.

   Whatever consciousness we provide is acted upon by this energy. Our thinking process is the action of using Its creative power!

3. The Law has many names, the most commonly heard are: principle, God, Spirit, universal mind, Oneness, wholeness, completion. Since It can only give back what is given to It, Its nature is considered ALL good – abundance, balance, beauty, freedom, joy, love, order, peace, power, unity, wholeness, wisdom.

4. We contact and direct this power through our believing words and thoughts. We don't ask or beg for It to do anything but accept that since we are of It, we already 'have'. Regardless of

57

whether we realise it or not the Law is always present as a presence. Accordingly, we know only Oneness.

5. Each of us is an individual expression of this all-encompassing One. By living in the consciousness of Oneness we dwell in what is commonly referred to as 'the kingdom of heaven'.

   The secret is in understanding that Law is working all the time. We unite with It by changing our thoughts to what we want and keeping them changed (i.e. we keep our mind focussed on **what we want**, not on what we **don't want**).

6. To succeed, to be fulfilled, we need to step over the barriers in our mind into a consciousness of 'having'. We need to remember that:

   - nothing happens by chance,
   - life is lived from within-out; it's not what happens 'out' there, but what we habitually think about, that manifests,
   - we live in an intelligent universe which is continually responding to our mental states.

7. Without any doubt whatsoever we need to know that our believing thoughts will manifest according to our conviction, just as surely as a seed planted in the ground will, in due course, sprout according to its nature.

8. Faith is the act of keeping our thoughts changed; it's the expectation and belief that our claim manifests exactly as we have envisioned it.

9. In sum, the Law is absolute and totally mechanical.

   With conviction and confidence we use our thoughts, words, feelings and beliefs to tell It what we wish to experience. We get rid of any barriers (fear, doubt, worry or concern), live our lives knowing that our desires are on their way, and then watch in amazement as they manifest in seemingly miraculous ways.

   We continually give thanks and enjoy life!

There is a rhythm in the Universe which, rightly understood, would resolve all conflict.

There is a peace in the Universe, a freedom of confusion which, rightly understood, would heal all troubles.

There is an all-encompassing love in the Universe which, rightly understood, would heal all emotional difficulties.

There is a creativity in the Universe which, rightly understood, would keep us whole and vitally active in expressing it.

Ernest Holmes and Willis H. Kinnear
A New Design for Living.

ABOUT THE AUTHOR

Neil Mence is an internationally-known author, speaker, teacher and mentor. His best-selling books include *SUCCESSFUL LIVING, NOTHING HAPPENS BY CHANCE* and *THE GREATEST STORIES EVER TOLD*.

Born in New Zealand, Neil has lived most of his life in Canada and recently moved to Europe. He has studied at Victoria University, Wellington, New Zealand, the University of Western Ontario, London, Canada, and City University, London, England. He holds a Doctor of Divinity degree from the Emerson Institute, California.

Combining more than 30 years' experience in the corporate world and new thought arenas of North America, Australia and Europe, he offers unique personal development and life-changing master classes to assist individuals and companies find their path, refocus priorities, and to transform, grow and realise their dreams.

"To me, life is all about going beyond limits, following your bliss, and achieving goals. I love helping people realise their true potential and to understand that happiness is not something out there to be achieved, but an inner flame just waiting to be realised."

Further information may be obtained from Neil's website: www.neilmence.com or by contacting him at info@neilmence.com.

Do you have a success story you'd like to share? Please contact me on info@neilmence.com

Herstellung und Verlag:
BoD - Books on Demand, Norderstedt
ISBN 978-3-7322-8496-20